Sing From Within

A guide to developing a dynamic singing voice using techniques used by the professionals

By
David Largie
PG Dip, BSc (Hons), MSc

David Largie

www.fast-print.net/store.php

Sing From Within: A guide to developing a dynamic singing voice using techniques used by the professionals
Copyright © David Largie PG DIP, BSc (Hons), MSc 2013

ISBN: 978-178035-486-6

All rights reserved

No part of this book may be reproduced in any form by photocopying or any electronic or mechanical means, including information storage or retrieval systems, without permission in writing from both the copyright owner and the publisher of the book.

The right of David Largie to be identified as the author of this work has been asserted by him in accordance with the Copyright, Designs and Patents Act 1988 and any subsequent amendments thereto.

A catalogue record for this book is available from the British Library

First published 2013 by
FASTPRINT PUBLISHING
Peterborough, England.

Sing From Within

Contents

Acknowledgments	5
Foreword	7
Preface	13
Chapter One Introduction	17

Chapter Two
    The Voice Instrument/Improve Your
    Vocal Control Singing Tips/Illustrations
	23

Chapter Three
    Breathing Technique/Vocal Support
    Singing Tips/Illustrations
	33

Chapter Four
    Relaxing the Throat/Resonance
    Singing Tips/Illustrations
	41

Chapter Five
   Increasing Vocal Range Singing Tips/
   Illustrations
	47

Chapter Six
   Creating Vocal Sounds, Textures;
   Vowel Pronunciation Singing Tips/Illustrations
	53

Chapter Seven
   Confidence, Performance Technique &
   Auditions Singing Tips/Illustrations
	61

Conclusion/A-Z of Singing	71

Acknowledgments

My thoughts, ideas, methods and successes have been greatly influenced by many individuals over the years; in terms of my experience and growth as a singing teacher. I am grateful for all good things seen and unseen, and everyone who has added to my knowledge, advancement, achievements and successes.

A very special 'thank you' is overdue to, in my opinion, the most inspiring, scholarly and competent vocal tutor that there is – ADE' and his Tae Jam Vocal School. Many thanks, brother, for being my mentor, and I hope the Creator continues to bless you and yours.

I also would like to thank my friends for putting up with me constantly talking about this book for singers. Their help in inspiring me and encouraging me is priceless - thank you.

David Largie

I dedicate this first book to my family who, as always, believed in me, supported me and pushed me to reach completion - Doreen, my eternal love, Mum, my life source, and my brothers and sisters Earl, Owen, Winston, Mary, Sonia and Lena. And, finally, my main motivators - my sons and daughters Akil, Nayler, Mandela, Kimarah, Kathleen and Kalyani. To all those I have neglected to thank, forgive me.

Foreword

It seems like only a few years ago that I was on my way to meet my future brother-in-law. My sister, Doreen, had decided that this was the guy she was going to marry. When I first met him, David Largie appeared larger than life and full of positive enthusiasm and energy. What I have since learned is that David is also a guru, and a master of connecting with and entertaining the souls of others through his singing, rapport, and entertaining. Most of all, he knows how to sing, what to sing, when to sing and why he sings, and he lives to share this, to help others discover the same for themselves.

There is nothing better than having a pleasant surprise.

David has not had it easy. He has had to work, gather his talents, make plans and carry out those plans. Adversity? You bet he's had that, in bucketloads, but that has not stopped him from singing live on national TV, singing live all over the country, and entertaining audiences with his voice and personality internationally.

We all still have so much to learn. Yet if we are curious, like children, we can learn to do practically anything well. To do this we have to be open-minded and remember that we should stay young, stay eager to learn. We never ever get to know it all. When you are green, you are growing; when you are ripe, you begin rotting. So stay green, stay sharp, and stay awake to the possibilities within you and within the world for you.

My first book, The 10-Second Philosophy, is a practical guide to happiness and success. It was already written and published internationally when David asked me to write the Foreword for his new book. But it was in the months that followed that I realised that there is a practical philosophy for happiness and success in singing and entertaining too. This is what David's book is about. There are, of course, many things that influence success and happiness as a singer, but the simple procedures that David shares within this book are a surefire way to help you become the greatest you. One thing that I vividly remember is how, when we spoke, David was able to simply de-mystify the keys to singing better and achieving success as a singer. He uses tools that are easy to follow and clearly enjoyable. Furthermore he is able, through this book and his coaching, to share simple steps that work.

David is a master at gaining rapport with others and helping them to identify what might be blocking them. He has worked with thousands of people, both in the English educational system and privately. He helps people to clarify their life's purpose and to remove the hidden barriers so that they can get the success and fun they desire. In addition, he has pioneered unique methods to help you establish ways forward that encourage improvement and fix the 'issues' that aspiring singers may have.

In this brilliant book, Sing From Within, David has distilled from his vast experience the simplest things that can change you. In order to go from beginner to good, or from good to great, we all need tools and the right guidance. We can be better than our pre-conditioning because we can re-condition ourselves for success. When we re-condition ourselves, we change.

When you change, everything will change for you. Because:

When you change, the world sees you differently.

When the world sees you differently, it treats you differently; then, everything will change for you.

Like the singer on a talent show, who is the same person before and after her debut performance, yet the world sees something in her that was always there but did not get the right level of exposure. Immediately that inner talent is revealed, the singer's life is changed.

Notice how this occurred though: the singer did something that allowed the world to see her inner gifts and talent; to see her as she really was. Then suddenly, overnight, the whole world treats the singer differently. The world wants to be part of the singer's life and world. The singer is fêted wherever she goes, yet in the same town and streets that she walked unnoticed the day before, she shines and everyone sees her authentic light.

Just as in life, when you are your authentic self you are better able to express yourself in song and to connect with others. Your song is able to move others because, within you, is a singer. And the singer within you resonates with the soul of the listener. Therefore it is vital to go through the emotion of singing, not just the motion of singing. Two singers sing; both are technically great, yet we connect with one instead of the other because we 'feel' them. Remember this whenever you sing.

I am delighted that David is in my life and I am thrilled that he is sharing his work with a larger 'audience' through the 'stage' of this book, bringing his work, insights and techniques to help others on a larger scale. Part of David's life purpose, similar to mine, is to help others to become all they can be. I believe that through this book he will have a massive impact on you, your career and the lives of others.

Don't just read this book; pay attention to the words, thoughts, questions, phrases and ideas that come from it. Then, most importantly, follow through and do what it recommends. Then who knows what dreams may come…

Derek Mills aka 'The Standards Guy'

Author of The *10-Second Philosophy: A Practical Guide to Releasing Your Inner Genius*

David Largie

Preface

The subject of improving singing and performance techniques, is an inexhaustible task that has generated many schools of thought about what makes a great singer.

The writing of Sing From Within is a labour of love that has been inspired by the many students that I have had the pleasure of teaching, and sharing this valuable knowledge with. The motivation to complete this book is based on the encouragement, and inspiration of many peers.

My love of singing began at a very young age; it was not, however, until I was twenty eight years old that singing, and understanding the techniques used, became my passion. This book is written with the intention of inspiring and motivating you to achieve your dreams of becoming a better singer, as well as adding to your overall knowledge and practical experience of using singing techniques.

This book will examine the importance of emotional expression, the interpretation of words, and singing techniques used to convey feelings. "Sing From Within" focuses on singing techniques used by professionals. This book also highlights the important elements of performance techniques.

"Sing From Within", is concise and contains only seven chapters, which are formulated to examine and offer you practical exercises and techniques to increase your singing ability, as well as providing you with instructions for incorporating the techniques into your singing style.

The best way to use this book is to firstly read it from Chapter one to through to Chapter seven, then select the various chapters that may be of particular interest to you, and then follow any instruction and advice given.

"Sing From Within", includes a summary at the end of each chapter, and a singing tip designed to offer you further useful pearls of wisdom.

Also included in this book, with the free Vocal Aerobics Warm-up exercise audio, is the download link for the Sing From Within SINGERS' ACTION PLAN.

This plan is designed to assist you practically in staying focused on improving your vocal ability, as well as building and maintaining confidence, deliberate emotional expression and, overall, professional performance attitude.

Singing from within and connecting with your emotions can be an exhilarating, self-satisfying and rewarding experience that can uplift any dreary day. When this energy is felt by an audience, the performance is then taken to another level of expression which is achieved only through pure intention and, inevitably, everyone enjoys the great performance and becomes a part of the great atmosphere.

David Largie

Chapter One

Introduction

The main purpose of writing this book is to share my experience, and knowledge, which I have acquired over ten years in regards to the 'Voice'.

The methods used are tried and tested, and have benefited both professionals, and semi-professionals alike. I have taught heat-winners on the Stars in Their Eyes TV program and I have been a contestant on The "X Factor" talent show.

Using your voice is like playing an instrument, 'Practice makes perfect'. Your progress and achievements are related to the commitments that you make in pursuit of excellence. So let's begin positively with the aim of growing in ability, getting better and better each day.

The level of your growth, development and improvement that you will achieve will depend on the amount of natural singing talent that you start out with, and the amount of time you invest in developing your singing ability; and the type of vocal exercises that you utilize and adapt. However, there are common qualities that are apparent in professional singers. Over the years, I have observed some of these qualities in students, and feel that they are important to mention at this stage, in the hope of identifying these qualities and thereby motivating and inspiring you to consciously apply yourself, thereby, ultimately reaping the rewards of focused Practice. Singers at all levels of professionalism and ability possess common characteristics that quickly become noticeable. These individuals make the teaching of singing a rewarding experience, allowing the tutor to be a part of their progress and development. Some of the qualities that are common to all serious-minded singers are:

- A burning desire;
- A passion for singing;
- Enthusiasm;
- Single mindedness;
- Self-motivation (to Practice regularly even when there are no gigs);
- Readiness to perform at every opportunity, to sing at the drop of a hat;
- A genuine interest in all aspects of singing;

- Reverence for great vocalist, past and present (in order to understand and appreciate the hard work, and effort needed to reach and maintain a profession standard).

Some individuals are born with a great-sounding voice; in my opinion, these individuals were lucky enough to have had their musical abilities encouraged and nurtured from a young age. However, most singers with beautiful voices have learned from past or current great singers through learning and studying their songs. In other words, they have applied and worked for years to create their own sound.

To develop and increase your confidence in singing and performing, it is vital to create and maintain a positive mental and physical environment (Please refer to Chapter Seven on Confidence, Performance Technique & Auditions)

We have a beautiful gift from nature that can help us to achieve this, namely our imagination. Humankind, has used its creative visualization to achieve the so-called impossible, such as building the pyramids, going to the moon, and the modern-day advancement of science and technology that has exceeded all previous prediction. I am sure that you too, have visualised the dream of performing before an exciting, alive and appreciative audience. This can become possible by developing your imagination to the extent of 'acting as if' you; have already achieved your dream performance (this will allow you to build up your self confidence, when facing a live audience).

Introduction

You can use your imagination to visualise your ideal feeling for singing and performing, as well as crowd response. For example, an image of yourself, electrifying a crowd, entertaining, performing at your best; basically, how you want to see yourself? By acting as if you had already achieved this before even beginning the rehearsal or gig, you are able to prepare your mind, for creating this very atmosphere.

To really develop quickly, you must immerse yourself with everything connected with being an artist. Ask yourself what type of lifestyle is common to professional singers, apart from the riches, and create that experience for yourself. Sing from within, with your mind, body and spirit. Use your singing voice as much as possible; sing for fun, sing to express yourself, sing to deliver a message, etc. In short, sing just because you can. Share your voice with the world and enjoy the ride. Celebrate all steps on the journey of getting better, no matter how small. Great singers stay flexible, they stay in shape, and they stay on the cutting edge of what they do and love.

Singing Tip 1

Imagine yawning while singing; this can help to relax the vocal chords and aid in singing better.

Summary of Chapter One

- Practice makes perfect, and consistency develops your confidence.

- Singers at all levels of professionalism and ability possess common characteristics that quickly become noticeable.

- To develop and increase your confidence in singing and performing, it is vital to create and maintain a positive mental and physical environment.

- You can use your imagination to visualise your ideal feeling for singing and performing, as well as crowd response; for example, an image of yourself exciting a crowd, entertaining, performing at your best - basically, how you want to see yourself.

- Through acting as if you had already achieved this, before even beginning the rehearsal or gig, you prepare your mind for creating this very atmosphere.

- Sing from your depths; your mind, body and spirit.
- Use your singing voice as much as possible; sing for fun, sing to express yourself, sing to deliver a message.
- To really develop quickly, you must immerse yourself in everything connected with being an artist.

Chapter Two
The Voice Instrument/Improve Your Vocal Control

There is endless technical knowledge available for research concerning how the voice works. It is not necessary to enter into a breakdown of how the voice works; this book is intended to focus on the application and expression of the singing voice. With this in mind, we begin with an analogy of the voice; your voice is a musical instrument that can be taught to produce high-quality sounds. Anyone can play a few notes on a piano, but to play beautifully requires a vast amount of Practice. As an instrument, your voice can be developed to levels of expression that are found in many of our professional singers. Singing correctly, and professionally, requires knowledge, Practice and application. The ability to use the voice to express human emotions is priceless, and an artist that can move you emotionally, can far outlive, and out-rank, the singers that can do all the wonderful vocal gymnastics.

The Voice Instrument/Improve Your Vocal Control

The sound that a musical instrument produces can loosely be defined as a tone. The sound of any other instrument playing middle C has the same pitch but has a different tone; this is what distinguishes one instrument from another. The voice like an instrument can also be taught to produce a variety of beautiful-sounding tones.

Concentrate on controlling the sound quality of the beginning, middle and end of every note to achieve excellence in tone quality. Tone placement, is developed from the shape of the mouth, and remember that the sound of the voice after warming-up is different from when the voice is cold; any fluids drunk should be at room temperature, to maintain tone quality. Keep the vocal cords lubricated at all times to maintain a relaxed, warm sound.

The beautiful sound that professional singers produce is a vital part of our lives and our very existence. This vibration of nature is, I believe, born within us all to a greater or lesser degree. The capacity for improvement is, therefore, available to us all. We may, with greater understanding of the mechanisms used by singers, increase the quality of the sound that we produce. Nature has provided us with a unique-sounding voice. For example, when you receive a phone call from a member of your family or from a well known friend; you will instantly recognize their voice's distinguishing characteristics, the subtle ways they pronounce the vowels, their embellishments, the sound of their speaking voice, whether breathy, harsh, soft, husky, deep, high, or bright; or their emphasis on particular words, etc. Our brain quickly calculates the qualities that define the voice, and who's calling. These identifiable aspects of voices can be utilized in singing, adding further dimensions such as emotional overtones and punctuation markers, or accents for various parts of a song. This book has been written to provide an easy approach to improving your singing and understanding of the voice, as well as highlighting the importance of interpreting songs emotionally.

To prepare properly for a gig, visualise yourself giving a dynamic performance, and include the crowd's reaction to your energy. The more imaginative and intense the vision, the greater will be the result. Prior to the performance, while warming-up, run through the scenes in your head and then strive to reproduce your dynamic vision. Properly prepare your voice by warming-up and warming-down.

This is achieved through a variety of vocal exercises. Which include: Tongue twisters, which are designed to assist in relaxing your facial muscles, soften your tone and warm-up the vocal chords. The constant practicing of tongue twisters will greatly improve your ability to use vowels effectively, create vocal textures and enhance the quality of your singing tone. Tongue twisters are also useful in getting your mouth around awkward combinations of words and phrases. There are a number of tongue twisters that can be used to Practice with, such as: 'Red lorry,

Yellow lorry', 'Unique New York', and 'Friendly Frank flips fine flapjacks', etc.

Vowel exercises are designed for better diction, pronunciation, and articulation. Just as the shape of the horn in a car defines the overall sound of the horn, so the shape of your mouth influences and characterizes the sound being produced. Muffled sounds are created by not opening the mouth enough to produce defined pronunciation. The vowels within a word dictate how the word sounds, and if you change the way you pronounce the vowels, you effectively change the sound. For example, in pronouncing a word like 'love', we can change it to 'lahve', or 'luhve', etc.; just by changing the spelling of a word you can alter the sound of the tone or the word being sung.

Most professional singers frequently sing along to scales as part of their warm-up routine. The main benefits of following scales are that they train the ear and enable you to stay familiar with pitch, thereby, developing the capacity to sing in tune and maintain your key. The standard middle C scale can be used initially, then more complex scales such as the pentatonic scales, which are mostly used in R&B and Rock tracks. You can progress to follow scales precisely, and it can also help to turn down the volume so you have to struggle to listen for the pitch; this can help you to focus more (refer to Vocal Aerobics CD for exercises).

Many voice specialist, and vocal coaches will agree, that in general, dairy products such as cheese, milk, ice cream, butter, yoghurt, chocolate, etc., create mucus, which will coat the larynx (voice-box) and affect its functions and overall tonal sound. Producers can clearly hear a difference in voice tone; as voice tones are affected by cold or fizzy drinks after warm up; they notice the subtle changes in the texture or sound of the voice.

Dry or brittle foods such as certain types of biscuits, chips, nuts, etc., should also be avoided. Most drinks are fine, but room-temperature water is best during performance or rehearsals as it keeps the throat or voice-box lubricated without additional irritants.

Posture

Good posture will assist in creating the physical ambience required for producing quality vocal sounds. If you should roll a sheet of paper into a cone, and blow through the narrow end, then this creates a sound. If then, you were to squeeze the centre of the cone; this would alter the sound by restricting the flow of air passing through it. Good posture begins with standing upright, shoulders back, chest slightly raised.

Visualise the posture of opera singers and you'll immediately see the almost regal stance they have while performing. I'm not suggesting that you shouldn't relax, dance and do your great moves, far from it, but always be aware of your overall physical pose.

Correct posture is necessary to allow the air/note to emerge. Stand with shoulders back, feet a couple of inches apart, chest slightly raised and head looking straight ahead about 90 degrees.

Incorrect posture while singing can also be a contributor to further tension and a restricted throat. Feeling relaxed all over is the basis of a good singing posture. Begin by standing in front of a long mirror practicing the correct posture. Your throat should be relaxed as though yawning; don't force the sound from your throat. Shoulders should not be hunched; this posture should be maintained. Be gentle with yourself, do not push or force the air from your diaphragm; remain natural and relaxed.

In general, keep your neck muscles and surrounding shoulder muscles relaxed. Do not tuck your chin in when trying to sing any low notes, or extend your head upward when trying to sing high notes.

Before moving on to the breathing technique (which offers support for the notes being song), it is worthwhile to Practice a variety of singing dynamics, using articulation of vowels, and various texture and sounds; such as: breathy...

Breathy, deep, bright, husky, bass tone, etc., to create emotional overtones.

Many great singers Practice in front of a mirror, rehearsing their set over and over again. An individual can also discover many strengths and weaknesses about their performance technique, and singing style. When faced with an audience, everything that you thoroughly rehearsed will become second nature.

Singing Tip 2

If you are paying for singing lessons, and you are not rehearsing regularly or using the techniques that you are being taught, then you are wasting time and money.

Invest your time wisely, in your quest, to improve your singing voice by practicing and warming up your voice daily.

The Voice Instrument/Improve Your Vocal Control

Summary of Chapter Two

- The voice when used as an instrument, can be taught to produce a variety of beautiful-sounding tones. Tone placement is developed from the shape of the mouth.

- Singing correctly, and professionally, requires knowledge, Practice and application.

- The artists that can move you inwardly, far outlives, and out-ranks, the singers that can do all the wonderful vocal gymnastics.

- The sound that a musical instrument produces can loosely be defined as a tone.

- Concentrate on controlling the sound quality of the beginning, middle and end of every note to achieve excellence in tone quality.

- Properly prepare your voice by warming-up and warming-down.

- Good posture assists in creating the physical ambience required for producing quality vocal sound.
- Many great singers Practice in front of a mirror, rehearsing their sets over and over again.

Chapter Three
Breathing Technique/Vocal Support

Breathing technique is one of the most important aspects of singing and is usually the cause of many problems that haunt singers of all abilities. Lack of correct breathing techniques can cause damage to your vocal chords, and in extreme cases, can cause permanent injury.

Breathing from your diaphragm when singing, gives the voice support, greater control and power. This will give you the capacity to sing for hours without straining your vocal chords.

If you observe a baby sleeping you will see the baby's abdomen as it contracts and expands (breathing diaphragmatically is the technical term for this). When we are relaxed we automatically breathe from our diaphragm without having to think about it.

Try lying flat on your back; then, for a few moments, think of something nice to relax you. Maybe you're on a beach, and the hot sun is beating down on you, etc. Now notice that you begin to breathe naturally, from your diaphragm (abdomen). The trick is to repeat this natural breathing process standing up. Professional singers and vocalists breathe from their diaphragms when singing. You can also try imagining that your diaphragm (just below the belly button) is like a balloon. When you breathe in, it's like putting air into the balloon, which will then inflate. When you breathe out your diaphragm, like the balloon, deflates again.

Snatch Breath

Snatch breath technique, is similar to that of the 'Breathing technique', with the added difference that the breath should be sucked in much more quickly, but in a shorter space of time.

Exercise

Whilst standing, place your hand onto your abdomen, apply a little pressure, with your hand on your stomach, then over the count of four, slowly take in a deep breath into your diaphragm. You should feel your hand, being pushed away by your diaphragm, if this is being executed correctly, then hold the air in your diaphragm again for the count of four. Release the air slowly and evenly over the count of four, by blowing the air out through your mouth, and returning back to normal breathing. Repeat this exercise a few times until it becomes easier and more natural (you should not breathe aggressively, or strain to take in or release air). Be aware that warm-ups should guide and reflect what you do when you sing. As the intensity of your warm-ups, will have an effect on the quality of your performance.

You should endeavor to sing and communicate using your diaphragm, as this will help you to develop quickly, as well as avoiding the strains of using the throat without the support of the diaphragm.

The "Sing From Within Vocal Aerobics warm-up Audio program" is best suited to these exercises; however, if needs are such, then you can use a metronome or something to keep a steady count.

Controlling your breathing

Professional singers always keep a reserve of air in the diaphragm. This is important to understand, as not keeping a reserve of air is also the cause of many potential singers not achieving a higher standard of vocal expression. We should take a breath when we need one, and try not to sing with the intention of getting to the end of the line, or getting rid of all the breath. Singing without releasing all the air combats the problem of running out of breath, and offers support and body for the notes being sung.

Breathing in a controlled manner, is vital for the developing artist and requires deeper breathing than in normal, everyday speech. Learning to control the amount of breath released whilst singing is dependent upon how you judge and pace yourself. Certain notes require more air than others, so we must Practice our breathing technique daily in order to develop an awareness of our tendencies and capacity. In addition, you will be grasping knowledge of how much air to release at a given time, when singing.

When breathing, we can use our imagination to help us along. For example: as you take a deep breath in, imagine that you are about to yawn; this causes you to relax and open the throat. Then, as you release the air, visualise yourself blowing softly into a balloon.

Practicing short hisses and panting can also develop breathing technique. Observe how the tummy muscles work automatically, with no effort on your part. Hissing and panting are both useful in control and strengthening of the diaphragm.

Breathe in, hold your breath for a count of four, and then release the air as a hiss, slowly and evenly, then increase this to: eight, twelve, sixteen, etc. Do this at various counts and then release the air for an equal length of time. This also builds stamina.

The quality of your breathing is a major factor for a controlled and professional quality to your voice.

Practice makes perfect; however, avoid practicing to the point of exhaustion. Keep the throat lubricated with plenty of room-temperature fluids. Singing at different volumes or projections can aid in developing further control.

Singing Tip 3

Professional singers always keep a reserve of air in the diaphragm.

Breathing Technique/Vocal Support

Summary of Chapter Three

- Breathing technique is one of the most important aspects of singing.

- Breathing from your diaphragm when singing gives the voice support, greater control and power, and the capacity to sing for hours on end without straining the vocal chords.

- You can also try imagining that your diaphragm (just below the belly button) is like a balloon. When you breathe in, it's like putting air into the balloon, which will then inflate. When you breathe out your diaphragm, like the balloon, deflates again.

- Practice makes perfect; however, avoid practising to the point of exhaustion. Keep the throat lubricated with plenty of room-temperature fluids.

Breathing Technique/Vocal Support

- You should take a breath when you need to, and try not to sing with the intention of getting to the end of the line, or getting rid of all the breath.

- Breathing in a controlled manner is vital for the developing artist and requires deeper breathing than in normal, everyday speech.

- Learning to control the amount of breath released whilst singing is dependent upon how you judge and pace yourself.

- Certain notes require more air than others, so you must practice your breathing technique in order to develop awareness of your tendencies and capacity, while at the same time grasping knowledge of how much air to release at a given time.

-

Chapter Four
Relaxing the Throat/Resonance

In laying the foundation for developing a professional singing voice; one on the most important aspects is preparation. Preparation involves the warming up of your vocal muscles before singing at full capacity. This will prevent damage to the vocal chords, thus enabling the voice to express and project itself fully. Similarly, to that of a singer, a professional athlete would not consider training, or competing without adequate warm up preparations.

Another important aspect in developing a beautiful singing voice is the opening and relaxing of the throat.

A common problem associated with potentially excellent singers is their inability to relax their throats while singing. This causes a number of problems, such as: restriction of vocal range, reduced tone quality and restricted projection; as well as possibly sounding sharp or ear-piercing. In order to fully appreciate the task of relaxing the throat, we should first be aware of a

Relaxing the Throat/Resonance

few of the main causes of, and contributors to, throat tension. These includes: lack of adequate vocal warm-ups before projecting the voice fully, over-articulation (too much exaggeration of lips and mouth movement), forcing air rather than using open mouth and using diaphragm to increase volume, and under-developed vocal muscles.

In developing some possible solutions we examine the act of yawning, which is an easy way of opening the vocal passage. Visualise yourself yawning. Feel as your throat opens up in preparation (the operation of yawning is useful for preparing you to sing). Try yawning, but don't open your mouth yet. Feel how the shape of your throat changes and expands. By singing like this you will open and relax the throat. Now say these vowels softly and slowly from your diaphragm. Relaxing the throat muscles will give you greater vocal control.

A	as in aid	A	as in apple
E	as in eat	E	as in ever
I	as in eye	I	as in is
O	as in owe	O	as in on
U	as in unit	U	as in super

The 'Vocal Siren' is another excellent vocal exercise for relaxing and opening the throat, because it takes you through your vocal registers from your chest voice to your head voice. You begin to realize your habits, where your voice cracks or breaks while passing through your vocal range (See Increasing Vocal Range Chapter five)

Start by adopting a good posture, then take a good breath into your diaphragm and sing 'ooh' at a comfortable, low note. Then move smoothly upwards to a comfortable, high note. Imagine a thermometer in front of you, and as you glide up the scale, so the mercury rises, and as you descend, visualise the mercury moving down the scale slowly until you are back to the note that you started with.

Singing Tip 4

Use tongue twisters regularly, expressing them softly and breathily to send warm air through the vocal chords, thereby, warming up the voice.

Relaxing the Throat/Resonance

Summary of Chapter Four

- Like a professional athlete, who would not consider competing or going all-out without adequate warm-ups, the professional singer, must use warm-up exercises to prevent damage to the vocal chords, and further, enable the voice to express and project itself fully.

- The opening and relaxing of the throat is another important aspect of developing a beautiful singing voice.

- In order to fully appreciate the task of relaxing the throat, you should first be aware of a few of the main causes of, and contributors to, throat tension.

- **These include** lack of adequate vocal warm-ups before projecting the voice fully, over-articulation (too much exaggeration of lips and mouth movement), forcing air rather than using open

Relaxing the Throat/Resonance

mouth and diaphragm to increase volume, and under-developed vocal muscles.

- The act of yawning is the easiest way of opening the vocal passage. Visualise yourself yawning. Feel as your throat opens up in preparation (the operation of yawning is useful for preparing you to sing).

- Try yawning, but don't open your mouth yet. Feel how the shape of your throat changes and expands. By singing like this you will open and relax the throat.

Chapter Five
Increasing Vocal Range

I have had the pleasure of teaching many students, that have a passion for learning and developing the voice, these individuals excel in their ability and knowledge of vocal techniques. A few of my students have progressed to becoming teachers themselves - for instance Adanta Beverley Dubidat and Miss Emma Mendez – and I now learn from them. This chapter on 'Increasing vocal range' is added courtesy of Miss Beverley Dubidat, who currently teaches privately within the West Midlands area (UK).

Increasing Vocal Range, By Beverley Dubidat.

'How do I increase my vocal range'? This question I have been asked many times. Over the years, I have heard many different vocal styles. My opinion is that, even though we are born with some natural ability, we have the capacity to increase our vocal range, as well as pitching, tone quality and overall vocal control. Vocal lessons and daily regimes will help to strengthen your diaphragm, thus increasing your control and clarity.

Everything we do has an effect on our vocals; the human voice, like an instrument, must to be cared for. Singing is a mind, body and soul thing; being united as one. The best singers, every part of their body tingles with the vibrations from their vocals as it comes from within.

Strengthening the 'Head Voice', will not necessarily, strengthen the 'Chest Voice', as they require different techniques. However, they are both important as the Head Voice will allow you to increase your upper vocal range, whereas, the Chest Voice will allow you to develop Mid and Lower Range.

Exercises

Here are a few exercises that I have used myself to improve and develop my vocal range, diaphragm, and pronunciation of vowels and consonants.

The first exercise is easier to understand if I say: 'Put your hand on your lower stomach and pretend to cough.' Feel what happens?

For this exercise we are going to use the consonants F, S and K.

Begin by breathing into your diaphragm steadily over a count of four, hold, and then begin (mimicking the same motion as above) 'FFFF' (like fun) 30 to 40 times. Continue on to 'SSSS' (as in Sir, and remember to breathe before you begin). Finally, 'KKKK' (like kite). These exercises are good warm-ups, as it will help you to find the right positioning for your voice.

Breathe into your diaphragm and project the vowel 'ah' (as in 'art') twice, then, take a breathe into the diaphragm, and hold the third 'ah', for a count of four. Continue, this 'ah' exercise and double it (to six), remembering to sustain the last 'ah' to the count of four. Increase this exercise in multiples of three, up to thirty.

Another great exercise for increasing the vocal range is to sing: 'mi me ma mo mu' on each note of the scale, ascending and descending, ascending and descending. For more variety you can also include other consonants such as: Fi, Fe, Fa, Fo, and Fu.

Practice your siren regularly (which involves singing from a low to a high note, and back again, in one smooth breathe flow). To become familiar with your vocal range, and tendencies, like the pitch at which your tone changes, this will be useful for creating your unique sounding voice.

When you explore your 'Head Voice', this will open up the senses within your mouth, face and head; resulting in a more colourful sound. In contrast, failure to exercise consistently, could lead to the loss of muscle tone, and make your voice sound lazy.

Singing Tip 5

Focus your voice as though singing across a crowded room, to build projection, strength and consistency.

Summary of Chapter Five

- With vocal lessons and daily regimes to strengthen the diaphragm, you will sing with more control and clarity.

- Everything we do has an effect on our vocals. I found this out whilst studying; also, singing is a mind, body and soul thing - you have to be in tune with your body.

- The best singers will tell you, that, while they are singing, every part of their body tingles with the vibrations from their vocals as it comes from within.

- Really explore your 'Head Voice', as this opens up the senses within your mouth, face and head, as well as resulting in a more colourful repertoire.

- Strengthening the head voice will, in turn, strengthen the chest voice. This is because, while

Increasing Vocal Range

singing at both extents of your range, the way the muscles are used are totally different - you no longer need your diaphragm to be busting with as much air, but to be releasing the air almost rhythmically and controlled.

Chapter Six
Creating Vocal Sounds, Textures and Vowel Pronunciation

The beautiful sounds that professional singers produce provide one of the priceless elements of our lives that nature has given us to enjoy. Singers motivate us, inspire us, and move us emotionally. Some of us are fortunate enough to be engrossed in music from an early age, and our musical abilities reflect this.

This wonderful vocal expression of nature is, I believe, born within all of us to a lesser or greater degree. The capacity to improve and produce vocal sound of the highest quality is dependent on a combination of factors related to vocal technique, such as correct use of breathing, vowels, articulation, vocal textures and vocal tones, as well as creating dynamics with vocal pressure.

Typically, vocal warm-up exercises comprise these main features:

Physical preparation: stretching arms and relaxing shoulders; neck-rolling relaxation exercise.

Breath preparation: breathing exercises from the diaphragm, and exercises for developing the control of sustaining of notes.

Voice preparation: vowel exercises; tongue twisters for relaxing the facial muscles.

Resonance: softening the tone through resonance, this relaxes and opens the throat.

Regular, short periods of exercises are preferable to occasional, long sessions. Although these exercises are designed to maintain a healthy voice and prevent problems, they should never be seen as a substitute for voice therapy. You should seek professional advice before starting on a vocal exercise programme, especially in the presence of throat discomfort or a change in voice quality.

Many voice teachers classify the expression of the voice from three main locations and these are:

"Chest Voice" is usually the voice that we talk in generally; this is felt vibrating in your chest and throat area. The chest voice has a deep rooted and full sound. By altering your vowel pronunciation and vocal resonance can also, enhance your tone and make you sound deeper making your voice sound lower.

The 'Middle Voice' is positioned in the upper chest, and it produces a higher-sounding pitch than the Chest Voice. The tone of the Middle Voice is bright and crisp; it is also the most favored technique in popular music.

'Head Voice' is the name given to the light, bell-like sound that the voice produces; you know when you are using your Head Tones, because it is felt in the nasal area of your head.

Falsetto

The falsetto voice is frequently used in Rhythm &Blues, and usually expressed at the end of phrases. It is also known as the 'Baby Voice' or 'False Voice'. Falsetto is executed with the Head Voice, and most men use this tone of voice, when singing along with a female or when they don't know how to go up in pitch. They tend to sound like they are hitting a pitch but not with any real power. The Bee Gees, Al Green, Luther Vandross and Mariah Carey all use the Falsetto technique, as this compliments a strong voice. In my experience, most men tend to shy away from using Falsetto because they say it does not sound masculine. On the other hand, quite a few women are hesitant to sing in chest voice because they say the sound is not as sweet as the head voice.

Vowel Pronunciation

Vowel pronunciation embodies the sounds produced from our voice-box, and this gives us the capacity to create tone/sound changes. We can produce a variety of

Creating Vocal Sounds, Textures and Vowel Pronunciation

colourful tones by changing the shape of our mouths and using different vocal pressures, as well as numerous additional dynamics. The subtle, warm, breathy tone used by many professional singers, seem to add emotional expression by highlighting certain words, are often overlooked and not heard. Take time out, and listen to some of the finer voices of yesterday and today and really listen to the pronunciation, the dynamics, the textures and quality of the voice. Does the singer use their Chest Voice or Head Voice? Or is it a combination? Does the singer use light or dark singing tones? Is the voice hard, or soft? Does it contain different volumes? What subtle and clear vocal sounds are you hearing? Really listen, and then add these qualities to your singing.

The shape of our mouths, as previously mentioned, characterizes and defines the sound. If we think and visualise the shape of our mouths in terms of north/south, east/west, then we can see and hear how we can manipulate the sound being produced by changing the shape of our mouths. This subtle fluctuation of vibrations influences the sound.

To enter competitions that require you to sound like a particular singer or successfully reproduce the singing styles of various artists, capturing their unique singing approach and sounding like them, is achievable through manipulation of vowels, colourful tones and articulation, etc.

Singing Tip 6

The sound of the voice after warming-up produces a different tone from when the voice is cold; any fluids drunk should be at room temperature, to maintain tone quality.

Creating Vocal Sounds, Textures and Vowel Pronunciation

Summary of Chapter Six

- Creating Vocal Sounds, Textures and Vowel Pronunciation.

- The capacity to improve and produce vocal sound of the highest quality is dependent on a combination of factors related to vocal technique, such as correct use of breathing, vowels, articulation, vocal textures and vocal tones, as well as creating dynamics with vocal pressure.

- Typically, vocal warm-up exercises comprise these four main features:

- Physical preparation: stretching arms and relaxing shoulders; neck-rolling for relaxation.

- Breath preparation: breathing exercises from diaphragm, and exercises for developing control of sustaining of notes.

- Voice preparation: vowel exercises; tongue twisters for relaxing the facial muscles.

- Resonance: softening the tone.

- Many singing teachers classify the expression of the voice from three main locations: Chest voice, Middle voice & Head voice.

- Vowel pronunciation embodies the sounds produced from our voice-box, and this gives us the capacity to create tone/sound changes. We can produce a variety of colourful tones by changing the shape of our mouths and using different vocal pressures.

- Regular, short periods of exercise are preferable to occasional, long sessions.

Chapter Seven
Confidence, Performance Technique & Auditions

How we think before a performance, will impact on how we perform. Nerves and stage fright usually associated with a performance should be looked upon as a natural mechanism for preparing you to do your best. Think positively prior to your performance beforehand. When analyzing your performance, start by acknowledging the good points first.

Study the professionals, and identify the common characteristics of a dynamic performance, then incorporate them into your performance. Practice in front of a mirror to help you see what the audience sees. Record yourself on video, analyse your performance and then make the relevant changes. In addition, get some constructive feedback from friends and family and make further adjustments. Remember,

Practice makes perfect and hard work develops confidence.

Ask yourself why you like a certain artist(s). List their qualities. 'I like ....'s performance because...', and highlight the aspects you like. Then add them to your performance. Yes, copy in your own style, say the common things said by performers, such as 'How you feeling?' Say it with meaning, like your favourite artists do, and say how great you feel to be there with them, and so forth...

With our imagination we can see ourselves performing at any level. So visualise yourself at the top. Nerves sometimes get the better of us; however, nerves are good; it's nature's way of keeping us on our toes. Stay focused! Your nerves are not there to make you fail, but to enhance your performance, use them to your advantage. If nerves are overwhelming you, take a deep breath in and try acting as if you are not nervous; a kind of reverse psychology. If you were not nervous you would feel like this; act like you are enjoying the moment. When you get an attack of nerves, try to imagine that you are your favorite singer, and this is just another great performance, that you are going to deliver. Additionally, if it is a large audience, then concentrate on a particular individual, and direct your performance to them.

Engross yourself in the musical moment; emotionally attach yourself to the words, express them, and make the song your own.

You can identify the important aspects of a performance, in order to master them; concentrate on the following elements:

- Entrance (upon entrance, appear relaxed and be confident; 'Strike a pose').
- Image; (what is unique about your appearance, attitude and overall look)
- Ability to conceal mistakes; (Improvise with a joke or statement, expression)
- Ability to conceal nerves; (act as if)
- Sincerity; (Sing From Within or Act as if)
- Relaxed and natural; (Enjoy the moment)
- Confident; (Feel the atmosphere, be yourself, enjoy!)
- Vocal technique; (Sing with awareness whilst incorporating various techniques)
- Microphone control; (Listen to yourself, control the volume going into the microphone, close to your mouth for quieter notes and slightly further away for louder ones)
- Choreography; (Get some help if needs be, and get well rehearsed, so it appears natural)
- Visual emotional expression; (Practice in front of a mirror, act, be natural)
- Projection; (Focus singing outwardly to the back of the venue)

- Contrast/dynamics; (Create variation the sound you are producing)
- Emotional Embellishment. (Focused enfaces on a particular words or phrase in order to create feelings, Sing From Within)

Auditions

For some individuals, just the very thought of an audition brings on a nervous reaction.

From sweaty palms, butter flies in the stomach, to the shaking and knocking of knees; and even to the extreme of a panic attack. To think, all this and you're not even backstage, waiting to perform in front of an audience! This tells us that how we think before, during and after a performance has everything to do with our experience and, ultimately, how our performance turns out. There is very little difference between an audition and a performance except that, in quantity, the mindset, dynamics, aim and energy remain the same - to entertain. If your voice is weak, let your performance be outstanding. If your performance is poor, let your singing amaze and emotionally move the audience. However, the ultimate is to produce an outstanding performance alongside an amazing singing voice.

Undoubtedly there are numerous things to consider with regard to auditions and, in my opinion, the main component is to truly prepare and do your best, giving your all to the audition or performance. If you are not selected then, irrespective of the level attained in a competition, you can always walk away feeling proud and, moreover, see it as a loss to the judges for not really listening, feeling, or being wise enough to recognise talent when it is evident.

Ask yourself; how would you perform if you weren't scared or self-conscious, or if you didn't lose your confidence? We can become slaves to habitually thinking about our feelings, ultimately this leads to under-performing. In contrast we can take control before during and after a performance by focusing on the content and expression of our performance, drawing only on positive past experiences or positive visualisation on the ideal performance.

Using our imagination and actually role-playing will, slowly but surely, create an alternative way of thinking that produces results when mentally and physically applied.

When we fail to prepare, we prepare to fail. There's also a tongue twister and confidence-builder that I share with my students regularly; it is that perfect preparation prevents poor performance. The only true answer is to Practice, Practice, Practice; basically, leave very little to chance.

See the previous chapter for ideas on the dos and don'ts of performance.

Design your stage performance - things to think about before your performance; How to enter, act confidently, be friendly, know what you are going to say, and how you are going to say it, walking on stage confidently strutting your stuff; your expressions for certain parts of the song. Think about your gestures, mannerisms and facial expressions for certain parts of the song. Think about, how your on-stage choreography will enhance your performance; the more you know what you will do on stage the more you will be able to fine-tune your stagecraft. Your confidence will begin to grow without you even realising it, and then you will find yourself always prepared to sing. So now, when someone puts you on the spot, before the nerves set in you will find yourself singing. Develop your whole stage show. Expect things to go wrong - the track on the CD jumping, the microphone screaming or, even worse, not working. The truth is, every performance is unique and has its own individual set of circumstances. Create scenarios for solutions to life's little performance surprises. I once dropped the mike at a very important showcase.

I swiftly picked up the mike and said: 'Aren't you guys lucky I'm a confident individual?' and smiled sarcastically before continuing my performance as though I had meant it. After the performance, I received praise from the audience, and club owners, agents and promoters offering me gigs, with no one mentioning the microphone.

Believe in yourself; build your confidence in performing through dedication, disciplined rehearsals, and repetition. This will ultimately allow your natural and developed talent to shine.

Singing Tip 7

Share your voice with the world and enjoy the ride. Celebrate all steps on the journey of getting better, no matter how small. Imagine inhaling a pleasant aroma, such as that of a rose, to really open your channels of vocal expression.

Summary of Chapter Seven

- The nerves and stage fright usually associated with a performance should be looked upon as a natural mechanism for preparing you to do your best.
- When analysing a performance, start by acknowledging the good points.
- If nerves are overwhelming you, try acting as if you are not nervous - a kind of reverse psychology.
- Get lost in the musical moment; emotionally attach yourself to the words, express them, interpret them, and make the words come alive.
- How we think before, during and after a performance has everything to do with our experience and, ultimately, how our performance turns out.

- There is very little difference between an audition and a performance except that, in quantity, the mindset, dynamics, aim and energy remain the same - to entertain.

- There are numerous things to consider with regard to auditions.

- Truly prepare and do your best, giving your all to the audition or performance. If you are not selected then, irrespective of the level attained in a competition, you can always walk away feeling proud and, moreover, see it as a loss to the judges for not really listening, feeling, or being wise enough to recognise talent when it is evident.

- The only true answer is to practice, practice, practice; basically, leave very little to chance.

Conclusion

Once you have achieved and comprehend singing techniques, and greater control. Your next crucial aspect is emotional interpretation of the song. When you become engrossed in the lyrics of a song and the emotional interpretation of it, you can be taken to levels of dynamics that can only be achieved through pure emotion. When you are singing the words of the songs, such as: 'I will always love you or 'The pain I feel for you', your thoughts should embrace the sentiment, of pain. Similarly, an actor will think in terms of how to realistically portray the role in which they are depicting; you too, have to act out the song that you are singing, and bring it to life. (please refer to Chapter seven on Confidence, Performance Technique & Auditions)

Many singers have commented on how the emotion of a phrase have assisted them in being able to reach certain high notes or in expressing particular

Conclusion

notes in an unusual way. Like singing from within, you and the song become entwined.

This is what I call singing without singing, which is not a conscious act but a state of unified emotional that transforms your song and makes for a truly moving experience for yourself and your appreciative audience.

As highlighted in Chapter six when we communicate with one another, we speak with a unique variation of sounds or tones. Nature has gifted us with a unique-sounding voice. We produce distinctive high and low pitches, fast and slow phrases, different vocal pressures, and we place emphasis on certain words, etc. These variations in sounds or tones defines us and makes us instantly recognizable as soon as they are heard by someone who knows us well.

Likewise, in singing and performing we must use contrasting themes, volumes, vocal pressures, embellishments, etc., to create moving performances, for example breathy notes can be used to convey warmth & project a feeling of intimacy with your audience. These will include levels of dynamics and versatility that, when expressing the story of the song, produce a performance that is unique to you. The professional artist uses a variety of vocal textures, volumes, pressures, vocal sounds, and pronunciation for highlighting certain words, accenting them.

In my opinion, singing should not only be about using the voice to convey human emotion, but should also encompass the mind, body and spirit.

Technique is all-important; however, to sing from pure emotion without any real effort is the ultimate aim, as though breathing. A great singer once said, when confronted with the prospects of not being able to sing, 'Singing is how I breathe'. That singer was Billie Holiday.

The choices of songs and artists that we recommend can be quite different from your natural tone and style of delivery and, therefore, more challenging. This stretches your capacity and adds tones. These additional tones, diction and pronunciation styles will enhance your ability to create a variety of sounds through the different shapes that your mouth makes when trying to reproduce a song precisely. This will add additional tones, layers and textures of sounds to your already-unique voice.

When we truly sing we are transported into another dimension, where we embrace the spirit of singing without technicality, just total expression of words and the spirit of the song.

The Music Business

After persevering and achieving your new, improved, dynamic voice, comes the development of your business understanding, in order to share your talent with the world and not get exploited out of your creative expression. The music business, like all businesses, has evolved over the years. For example in the 60s, 70s and 80s Record companies A&R (Artiste &

Conclusion

Repertoire) scouted for talent; wandered the cities near and far, looking for the next superstar or Sensational Band. A friend of a scout could discover an individual by overhearing him or her singing on a train or bus.

Sadly, those days are long gone; these days, securing a recording deal, involves self promotion, networking and undying persistence; as today's music industry demands that singers are involved in all aspects of their career, from writing to developing their own creative image. You will need to become familiar with all aspects of the music business. To increase your awareness for specific information on the music industry in terms of: securing a recording deal, production deal, signing to a Labels, Artiste & Repertoire (A&R) contacts, as well as general networking, the internet is a good place to start.

There is no substitute for a good manager, for they can dramatically enhance your career and change your life. Do as much research as possible to find one that meets your specific requirements, for a manager would only be interested in you, once you can prove that you are a marketable product.

Finally the best advice that can be given to any aspiring professional musician is to, first and foremost, do it for yourself. Learn as much as you can, do as much as you can, make as many contacts as you can and, most importantly, Practice, Practice, Practice; prepare and perfect your talent and ability.

Copyrighting your songs

Initially, the so-called 'poor man's copyright' will suffice. This involves inserting the written song or hard copy into an envelope and then posting it to your address. On its arrival, do not open the envelope. Keep it in a safe place, to be presented if someone uses your material without your permission. The date stamped at the post office represents the date it was registered. However, the most secure way is to copyright your songs with an industry society, such as Performing Rights Society (PRS), or American Society of Composers, Authors and Publishers (ASCAP).

A to Z of Singers' advice

A = Articulate. When we communicate we pronounce our words in a particular way in speech or singing. Professional singers manipulate sound using tone changes, vowel variation and varying textures.

B = Breathing Technique. This is all-important, and professional singers usually take air into their diaphragm.

C = Communicate the song. Tell a story; choose to be the best you can be.

D = Diaphragmatic breathing. This consists of controlling airflow, with speed and evenness. Imagine that your diaphragm, which is found just below the belly button, is like a balloon; it takes in air, filling also

Conclusion

the lower part of your lungs. Then release the air slowly.

E = Express yourself. Make the words come alive and tell a story. Strive to become emotionally-charged as you interpret the song and your audience will become putty in your hands as you take them through the highs and lows of your performance.

F = Focus, Focus, Focus. Focus to become the best that you can be. Focus on your vocal technique, focus on your emotional expression, focus on your performance, and focus, on becoming the song that you sing.

G = Go for it. After hours and hours of practicing, the only thing left for you to do is to strut your stuff and perform your heart out.

H = Hear the notes in your head before singing them. The more defined the notes or melody are, the more precise the expression. Don't guess at the notes or pitch.

I = Improve, improve, improve. Improve daily; eat, sleep and dream of getting better. Six months, or even a year, of intense focus on improving your singing will be far more effective than periodical and inconsistent practicing.

J = Judge. Judge your own vocal technique, judge your expressions, judge your performance; become your own critique, while striving to become the best that you can.

Sing From Within

K = Knowledge is power. Lack of knowledge leaves you powerless to correct mistakes or develop a professional stage performance, but knowledge will allow you to performance at your best.

L = Love your voice. Appreciate your uniqueness and really listen to yourself. Really love the songs that you sing.

M = Motivation. When there are no shows available, or when you are feeling uninspired about the sound of your voice, celebrate even the smallest of successes.

N = Never let others define your future. Develop a plan of action, and never give in.

O = Open mouth expression. Use your mouth to create the sounds, with subtle and dramatic vowels and consonants characterizing the tone.

P = Perfect preparation prevents poor performance.

Q = Quietly. Sit quietly and use your powers of imagination to visualise where you truly want to be. Picture the audience screaming out your name.

R = Raise your game. Push yourself; ask yourself how you would perform if you weren't afraid, and act that way until it becomes an actual performance; and realize your full potential.

S = Sing, Sing, Sing. Sing when you are happy, sad, excited, or bored in general. Sing for pleasure, and the joy it brings; let your singing voice flow naturally. Every time you sing be relax and feel at ease with yourself.

Conclusion

T = Tone. Variations in tone add colour and textures which make a singing voice dynamic and avoid monotony or monotone.

U = Uniquely sounding voices. We all have elements of uniqueness within our voices that individualises us and defines us, and separates us from other singers.

V = Visualise. Visualise yourself exciting a crowd; the more detailed your imagination, the more you will produce the desired effect. You will find yourself actually and consciously exciting them.

W = Win it. You've got to be in it to win it or benefit from it. Perform regularly to build experience and professionalism.

Y = Yes! You Can Sing From Within. Exercise your voice daily with the 'Sing From Within Vocal Aerobics Audio Program'. You must sing all the time. Yes, sing just because you can. Don't yield to the temptation of becoming lazy.

Z = Zenith is your limit. Your zeal will produce the results you put into it, as hard work will develop your confidence.

To receive a free copy of the Sing From Within vocal aerobics exercise audio.

Please visit https://www.singfromwithin.com and enter this unique reference code MAUBEICLA139724

Singing Action Plan

*S*ing From Within

> Sing from within, with your mind, body and spirit, use your singing voice as much as possible (Chapter One).
>
> Use Emotional Embellishment (Focused enfaces on a particular words or phrase in order to create feelings, Sing From Within, (Chapter Seven).
>
> Exercise your voice daily with the 'Sing From Within Vocal Aerobics Audio Program'. You must sing all the time. Yes, sing just because you can.
>
> Don't yield to the temptation of becoming lazy. (A to Z of Singers' advice)

Conclusion

*I*magine & visualise

To prepare properly for a gig, visualise yourself giving a dynamic performance, and include the crowd's reaction to your energy. (Chapter One)

Imagine that you are your favorite singer, and this is just another great performance, that you are going to deliver. (Chapter Seven)

Raise your game. Push yourself; ask yourself how you would perform if you weren't afraid, and act that way until it becomes an actual performance; and realize your full potential.(A to Z of Singers' advice)

*N*arrate your song

Engross yourself in the musical moment; emotionally attach yourself to the words, express them, and make the song your own. (Chapter Seven)

Use visual emotional expression (Practice in front of a mirror, act, be natural)

Project (Focus singing outwardly to the back of the venue). Chapter Seven

Use contrast/dynamics (Create variation in the sound you are producing).

(Chapter Seven)

Emotionally Embellish (Focused enfaces on a particular words or phrase in order to create feelings, Sing From Within,

(Chapter Seven).

Conclusion

*G*auge your performance

> Breathing in a controlled manner, is vital for the developing artist, and requires deeper breathing than in normal, everyday speech. Learning to control the amount of breath released whilst singing is dependent upon how you judge and pace yourself (Chapter Three).
>
> Certain notes require more air than others, so you must Practice your breathing technique in order to develop awareness of your tendencies and capacity, while at the same time grasping knowledge of how much air to release at a given time (Chapter Three).
>
> Believe in yourself; build your confidence in performing through dedication, disciplined rehearsals, and repetition. This will ultimately allow your natural and developed talent to shine (Chapter Seven).

Express yourself

> Use your singing voice as much as possible; sing for fun, sing to express yourself, sing to deliver a message. (Chapter One)
>
> Express yourself. Make the words come alive and tell a story (A to Z of Singers' advice).
>
> The professional singer must use warm-up exercises to prevent damage to the vocal chords, as this will enable the voice to express and project itself fully (Chapter Four).

Conclusion

*R*ehearse & re-invent

An individual can also discover many strengths and weaknesses about their performance technique, and singing style. When faced with an audience, everything that you thoroughly rehearsed will become second nature (Chapter Two).

The only true answer is to practice, practice, Practice. Basically, leave very little to chance (Chapter Seven).

Think positively prior to your performance beforehand. When analyzing your performance, start by acknowledging the good points first (Chapter Seven).

Stage Presence, Act as if

Study the professionals, and identify the common characteristics of a dynamic performance, then incorporate them into your performance. Practice in front of a mirror to help you to see what the audience sees. (Chapter Seven)

Develop your whole stage show. Expect things to go wrong - the backing track on the skipping, the microphone screaming or, even worse, not working. The truth is, every performance is unique and has its own individual set of circumstances... (Chapter Seven).

Stay focused! Your nerves are not there to make you fail, but to enhance your performance, use them to your advantage (Chapter Seven).